Team Spirit

THE PITTSBURGH PIRATES

BY

MARK STEWART

Content Consultant
James L. Gates, Jr.
Library Director
National Baseball Hall of Fame and Museum

NORWOOD HOUSE PRESS
CHICAGO, ILLINOIS

Norwood House Press
P.O. Box 316598
Chicago, Illinois 60631

For information regarding Norwood House Press, please visit our website at:
www.norwoodhousepress.com or call 866-565-2900.

Editor: Mike Kennedy
Designer: Ron Jaffe
Project Management: Black Book Partners, LLC.
Special thanks to Jan Paul Matthews.

Library of Congress Cataloging-in-Publication Data

Stewart, Mark, 1960-
  The Pittsburgh Pirates / by Mark Stewart ; content consultant James
L. Gates.
       p. cm. -- (Team spirit)
  Summary: /"Presents the history, accomplishments and key personalities of
the Pittsburgh Pirates baseball team. Includes timelines, quotes, maps,
glossary and websites"--Provided by publisher.
  Includes bibliographical references and index.
  ISBN-13: 978-1-59953-172-4 (library edition : alk. paper)
  ISBN-10: 1-59953-172-0 (library edition : alk. paper)
  1. Pittsburgh Pirates (Baseball team)--History--Juvenile literature.
I. Gates, James L. II. Title.
GV875.P5S837 2008
796.357'640974886--dc22
                                                        2007040058

3586

COVER PHOTO: The Pirates celebrate a win during the 2005 season.

Table of Contents

SPORTS WORDS & VOCABULARY WORDS: In this book, you will find many words that are new to you. You may also see familiar words used in new ways. The glossary on page 46 gives the meanings of baseball words, as well as "everyday" words that have special baseball meanings. These words appear in **bold type** throughout the book. The glossary on page 47 gives the meanings of vocabulary words that are not related to baseball. They appear in ***bold italic type*** throughout the book.

Meet the Pirates

Baseball fans love to watch good hitting. Throughout their long history, the Pittsburgh Pirates have given the fans what they love. The team has a long list of batting champions and league-leading **sluggers**. It is a *tradition* that today's players work hard to continue.

The Pirates do more than hit, of course. They have had many *extraordinary* pitchers, fielders, and baserunners. The Pirates pride themselves on playing good **all-around** baseball, and they have the championship trophies to prove it.

This book tells the story of the Pirates. They have made a lot of history since joining the **National League (NL)** in the 1800s. They play to win from the beginning of the season to the end. When you wear a Pirates uniform, you are expected to do nothing less.

The Pirates congratulate each other after a victory in 2007.

Way Back When

The Pirates began their baseball life in 1882 as the Pittsburgh Alleghenys. They were members of a new league, the **American Association (AA)**, which had also formed in 1882. The Alleghenys were named after the mountains near Pittsburgh. They had good players and loyal fans. In 1887, the team was invited to join the NL. A few years later, the Alleghenys changed to a more exciting name, the Pirates.

By 1900, the Pirates were owned by Barney Dreyfuss. He also owned an NL team in Louisville, Kentucky. Dreyfuss decided to end the Louisville team, but first he traded his best players to Pittsburgh. That would never be allowed today. Back then, it was seen as "smart business."

The players in that lopsided trade included outfielder Fred Clarke and Honus Wagner, the game's greatest young star.

The Pirates won the **pennant** three years in a row starting in 1901. In 1903, they played the Boston Americans in the first modern **World Series**. Six years later, Pittsburgh won the World Series. The team defeated the Detroit Tigers in a showdown between Wagner and Ty Cobb, the best player in the **American League (AL)**.

The Pirates were NL champions again in 1925 and 1927. Those clubs had strong hitters, including Pie Traynor, Kiki Cuyler, and Glenn Wright, and later the Waner brothers, Paul and Lloyd. Pittsburgh finished in second place five times in the years that followed, but the team did not return to the World Series. The Pirates sank to the bottom of the league after World War II. The only reason many fans came to the ballpark was to watch the amazing power hitting of Ralph Kiner.

By the 1960s, the Pirates had rebuilt their club around pitching and fielding. Vern Law, Bob Friend, and Roy Face were among the top pitchers in the league. Roberto Clemente, Bill Virdon, Dick Groat, and Bill Mazeroski gave the team great defense and

LEFT: Fred Clarke, Tommy Leach, and Honus Wagner—the leaders of the Pirates in the early 1900s. **ABOVE**: The Waner brothers ride the shoulders of teammate Big Jim Weaver.

dependable hitting. The Pirates won the World Series in 1960 and had several more winning seasons during the **decade**. In 1971, Clemente led a new group of stars to another pennant. He teamed with Willie Stargell, Manny Sanguillen, Dave Cash, Richie Hebner, and Al Oliver to bring another championship to Pittsburgh.

In 1979, it was Stargell's turn to lead the team to a championship. Known by his younger teammates as "Pops," he played like a kid, and his **enthusiasm** rubbed off on the Pirates and their fans. With help from Bill Madlock and Dave Parker, Pittsburgh danced its way to World Series glory to the beat of "We Are Family," a popular **disco** song.

In the 1980s and 1990s, the Pirates did not have a lot of money to spend on **free agents**. They still had a great team, thanks to their clever manager, Jim Leyland, and **All-Stars** such as Doug Drabek, John Smiley, Bobby Bonilla, Jay Bell, Andy Van Slyke, and Barry Bonds. The Pirates came within one out of reaching the World Series in 1992. Unable to keep its best players, the club began rebuilding for the 21st **century** with new stars and a new stadium.

LEFT: Roberto Clemente, Pittsburgh's greatest star during the 1960s.
ABOVE: Barry Bonds, who developed into one of baseball's best players with the Pirates.

The Team Today

After their great seasons in the 1990s, the Pirates struggled for many years. Young stars such as Aramis Ramirez, Jason Kendall, and Jason Schmidt were asked to carry a heavy load. In the end, they were unable to do so, and the team fell on hard times.

The Pirates decided to rebuild their club around pitching. The team **drafted** players with strong arms, and it showed great *patience* as they developed. Soon fans were cheering for a whole new group of stars, including pitchers Ian Snell, Tom Gorzelanny, and Matt Capps. Hitters Jason Bay, Adam LaRoche, and Freddy Sanchez also made important contributions.

The Pirates are again playing exciting baseball and putting quality players on the field. They root for each other and learn from one another. With a core of young stars, the team has the building blocks it needs for a return to glory.

Jose Bautista is greeted at home plate by Freddy Sanchez, Jason Bay, and Xavier Nady during the 2006 season.

Home Turf

For more than 60 years, the Pirates played in Forbes Field. The ballpark was named after a general who won important battles near Pittsburgh in the 1700s. It was an enormous stadium, and the outfield walls were far away from home plate. Players found it hard to hit home runs, but doubles and triples came very easily.

The Pirates moved to Three Rivers Stadium in 1970. It was built in a spot where three rivers—the Monongahela, Allegheny, and Ohio—come together. After 31 seasons there, the team moved to a new ballpark on the Allegheny River called PNC Park. It has beautiful arches like Forbes Field, plus great views of the Pittsburgh skyline and waterfront.

BY THE NUMBERS

- *The Pirates' stadium has 38,496 seats.*
- *The distance from home plate to the left field foul pole is 325 feet.*
- *The distance from home plate to the center field fence is 399 feet.*
- *The distance from home plate to the right field foul pole is 320 feet.*
- *The right field wall is 21 feet high in honor of Roberto Clemente, who wore number 21.*

The right field wall can be seen in this picture of Pittsburgh's stadium.

Dressed for Success

Back when the team was called the Alleghenys, the players wore striped uniforms. Their fans called them the Potato Bugs, after a brightly striped insect. In the first half of the 1900s, Pittsburgh's main color was dark blue, often with red trim added.

The Pirates started wearing their familiar black and gold colors in 1948. In 1957, they began featuring a uniform with a sleeveless vest. The team kept that style right through the 1960s. In recent years, Pittsburgh used a similar style.

In the 1970s, the Pirates switched back to a regular uniform but

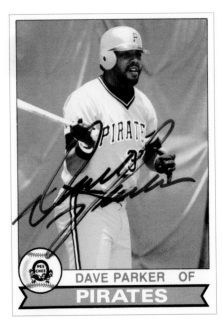

used many different combinations of black, gold, and white. Some days they wore black jerseys and pants with a gold hat. Other days they wore gold jerseys and pants with a black hat. They also wore black and gold pinstripes. In 1985, the Pirates switched to a uniform that looked like their first black and gold model.

Dave Parker in the team's all-gold uniform of the 1970s.

UNIFORM BASICS

The baseball uniform has not changed much since the Pirates began playing. It has four main parts:

- a cap or batting helmet with a sun visor
- a top with a player's number on the back
- pants that reach down between the ankle and the knee
- stirrup-style socks

The uniform top sometimes has a player's name on the back. The team's name, city, or *logo* is usually on the front. Baseball teams wear light-colored uniforms when they play at home and darker styles when they play on the road.

For more than 100 years, baseball uniforms were made of wool *flannel* and were very baggy. This helped the sweat *evaporate* and gave players the freedom to move around. Today's uniforms are made of *synthetic* fabrics that stretch with players and keep them dry and cool.

Jose Castillo shows off the team's 2007 home uniform.

We Won!

The Pirates played in the first modern World Series in 1903. Many of their stars were injured, and they lost to the Boston Americans. Pittsburgh fans were eager for their team to challenge again for a championship. They got their chance in 1909.

The Pirates won the pennant easily that season, thanks to their great star Honus Wagner. He led the NL in batting for the fourth year in a row and was the only player in the league to

CAMNITZ PITTSBURG

reach 100 **runs batted in (RBI)**. Player-manager Fred Clarke and outfielder Tommy Leach scored many of those runs. Howie Camnitz, Vic Willis, and Babe Adams were the team's best pitchers. In the World Series, Pittsburgh beat the Detroit Tigers for the championship.

The Pirates returned to the World Series in 1925, against the Washington Senators. It took seven games to decide the winner. Pittsburgh was led by two speedy outfielders, Max Carey and Kiki Cuyler, and hard-hitting infielders Pie Traynor and Glenn Wright. The Pirates lost three of the first four games but fought back

Harold "Pie" Traynor

LEFT: Howie Camnitz, one of the team's top pitchers in the early 1900s.
RIGHT: Pie Traynor
BELOW: A trading card shows the celebration after the 1960 World Series.

to tie the series. In Game Seven, they were behind until the seventh inning. Traynor tied the game with a triple, and Cuyler doubled home the winning runs.

The Pirates played in the World Series again in 1927, but they were swept by the powerful New York Yankees. Pittsburgh fans had to wait until 1960 for their next chance at a title. The Pirates faced the Yankees again, but this time they beat New York in seven wild games. Shortstop Dick Groat, outfielder Roberto Clemente, and pitchers Vern Law and Roy Face starred for the Pirates. The winning hit came with the score tied 9–9 in the bottom of the ninth inning. Bill Mazeroski drove a ball over the left field wall to give Pittsburgh a dramatic victory.

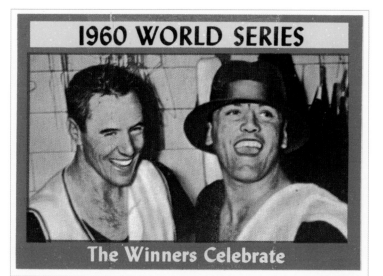

1960 WORLD SERIES

The Winners Celebrate

The Pirates won championships again in 1971 and 1979. Both times they played the Baltimore Orioles, and both times the Orioles were ahead in the series. In 1971, Clemente and pitcher Steve Blass led their **comeback**. In Game Seven, Blass pitched a gem and won 2–1. Clemente sparked the offense and gave the Pirates the runs they needed to secure the victory.

In 1979, slugger Willie Stargell and **relief pitcher** Kent Tekulve helped the Pirates win the World Series in seven games. The team also got great pitching from Bert Blyleven and John Candelaria. For the second time in their history, the Pirates won the championship after trailing three games to one.

ABOVE: Steve Blass pitches against the Baltimore Orioles in the 1971 World Series.   **RIGHT**: Willie Stargell rounds third base after hitting a home run in Game Seven of the 1979 World Series.

Go-To Guys

To be a true star in baseball, you need more than a quick bat and a strong arm. You have to be a "go-to guy"—someone the manager wants on the pitcher's mound or in the batter's box when it matters most. Fans of the Pirates have had a lot to cheer about over the years, including these great stars …

THE PIONEERS

HONUS WAGNER   Shortstop

• BORN: 2/24/1874 • DIED: 12/6/1955 • PLAYED FOR TEAM: 1900 TO 1917

Honus Wagner was a powerful hitter, fast runner, and excellent

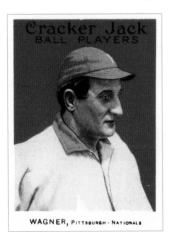

WAGNER, PITTSBURGH - NATIONALS

fielder—and the best player in the NL in the early 1900s. Wagner, who won eight batting championships, loved baseball so much that he continued to play for local teams in Pittsburgh until he was 50.

FRED CLARKE   Outfielder

• BORN: 10/3/1872   • DIED: 8/14/1960
• PLAYED FOR TEAM: 1900 TO 1911 & 1913 TO 1915

Fred Clarke did not have tremendous natural talent. However, he was one of the smartest men in the game. Clarke used his brains, bat, and legs to become the best left fielder—and manager—of his time.

ABOVE: Honus Wagner   **RIGHT**: Paul and Lloyd Waner

PIE TRAYNOR

- BORN: 11/11/1898   • DIED: 3/16/1972
- PLAYED FOR TEAM: 1920 TO 1935 & 1937

When Pie Traynor joined the Pirates, third base was a position played by **agile** fielders. Traynor was one of the first third basemen who was also a feared hitter.

PAUL WANER   Outfielder

- BORN: 4/16/1903   • DIED: 8/29/1965
- PLAYED FOR TEAM: 1926 TO 1940

Paul Waner and his brother, Lloyd, were two of the best outfielders in the NL. Paul won three batting championships for the Pirates. He was also a good right fielder with a powerful arm.

RALPH KINER   Outfielder

- BORN: 10/27/1922
- PLAYED FOR TEAM: 1946 TO 1953

Horseshoe-shaped Forbes Field could be a difficult park for home run hitters. Ralph Kiner was able to pull balls down the left field line, where the fence was closer to home plate. Soon, that area became known as "Kiner's Korner." Kiner led the NL in home runs in his first seven seasons with the Pirates.

MODERN STARS

ROBERTO CLEMENTE   Outfielder

- BORN: 8/18/1934   • DIED: 12/31/1972
- PLAYED FOR TEAM: 1955 TO 1972

Roberto Clemente played baseball with great style. He won four batting championships and 12 **Gold Glove** awards, and was the league's **Most Valuable Player (MVP)** in 1966. The beloved star died while delivering relief supplies to earthquake victims in Nicaragua.

BILL MAZEROSKI   Second Baseman

- BORN: 9/5/1936   • PLAYED FOR TEAM: 1956 TO 1972

Bill Mazeroski hit the home run that won the 1960 World Series, but he was best known for his defense. "Maz" rarely made an error, and no one was better at completing double plays.

WILLIE STARGELL   Outfielder/
First Baseman

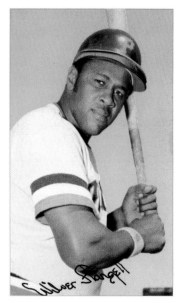

- BORN: 3/6/1940   • DIED: 4/9/2001
- PLAYED FOR TEAM: 1962 TO 1982

The secret to Willie Stargell's success was staying relaxed. Few players enjoyed the game more than he did. Even fewer could hit the ball as far. In 1979, at the age of 39, "Pops" was the MVP for the season, **National League Championship Series (NLCS)**, and World Series.

DAVE PARKER
Outfielder

- BORN: 6/9/1951
- PLAYED FOR TEAM: 1973 TO 1983

Dave Parker was nicknamed the "Cobra" for the way he *uncoiled* his body when he swung. He was one of baseball's best all-around players, and one of the toughest. In 1978, Parker played with a broken jaw and won the NL MVP award.

BARRY BONDS — Outfielder

- BORN: 7/24/1964
- PLAYED FOR TEAM: 1986 TO 1992

Barry Bonds began his career with the Pirates at the age of 21. He led the NL in **slugging average** twice with Pittsburgh and became the best left fielder of his *generation*.

JASON BAY — Outfielder

- BORN: 9/20/1978
- PLAYED FOR TEAM: 2003 TO 2008

The Pirates got Jason Bay as a **throw-in** in a trade with the San Diego Padres. Once the team realized his incredible talent, Bay became one of the best all-around players in baseball. He was named NL **Rookie of the Year** in 2004.

TOP LEFT: Roberto Clemente
BOTTOM LEFT: Willie Stargell
ABOVE: Barry Bonds

On the Sidelines

The Pirates have had many *remarkable* managers in their history. In the 1890s, Connie Mack roamed the dugout. He would go on to win 3,731 games in his career. In the early 1900s, Fred Clarke was Pittsburgh's left fielder and manager. He loved to steal bases and told his players to do the same. Clarke led the team to the NL pennant each year from 1901 to 1903, and again in 1909.

Bill McKechnie managed the Pirates in the mid-1920s. He was one of the smartest men in baseball. He led Pittsburgh to the championship in 1925. Another smart manager was Danny Murtaugh. He was named manager of the Pirates four different times. Under Murtaugh, the team won the World Series in 1960 and 1971.

The Pirates' manager in 1979 was Chuck Tanner. He made great mid-season moves that gave the team the boost it needed to win the pennant. In 1986, Jim Leyland took over. He molded a young team into a winner and set a high *standard* for the managers who followed him.

Chuck Tanner responds to cheers from the Pittsburgh fans during the 1979 World Series. The Pirates beat the Baltimore Orioles for the championship.

One Great Day

No one thought the Pirates had a chance in the 1960 World Series. The New York Yankees had some of the greatest stars in baseball. Few fans outside of Pittsburgh knew the players on the Pirates. The Yankees showed their might in their three victories.

They outscored the Pirates 38–3 in those games.

But the Pirates won three games, too. Their victories came by scores of 6–4, 3–2, and 5–2. The seventh game of the World Series was played in Pittsburgh, and it seesawed back and forth. The Pirates led 4–0 after four innings, with **starting pitcher** Vern Law looking strong. The Yankees came back to take the lead 5–4 in the sixth inning. They scored two more runs to make it 7–4 in the eighth.

LEFT: Bill Mazeroski heads for home after his World Series home run.   **RIGHT**: "Maz" was better known for his fielding than his hitting.

The Pirates stormed back. A couple of lucky bounces and a home run by catcher Hal Smith put them ahead 9–7. When the ninth inning started, Pittsburgh needed three outs for the championship. The Yankees would not give up. They scratched out two runs to tie the score 9–9.

Bill Mazeroski, the Pirates' light-hitting second baseman, stepped into the batter's box to begin the bottom of the ninth inning. He faced Ralph Terry, a very tricky pitcher. Terry threw a fastball, and Mazeroski let it go for ball one. Terry's next pitch was a high **slider**. Mazeroski met the ball with the fat part of his bat and watched as his drive soared over the fence in left field.

The crowd at Forbes Field was caught off guard. They went from dead silence to mad cheering. It took Mazeroski a moment to realize that he had just won the World Series with one swing. By the time he rounded the bases, he had a wide grin on his face. Fans and teammates rushed on the field to congratulate Mazeroski as he neared home plate. It was the greatest day ever for Pittsburgh baseball.

Legend Has It

Were the Pirates the first team to wear batting helmets?

LEGEND HAS IT that they were. Branch Rickey, who ran the team's business in the 1950s, decided that all of the Pirates should wear helmets. He put Charlie Muse, who worked for the club, in charge of designing them. The Pirates began wearing their helmets in 1952. At first, their opponents teased them. However, within a few years, every player in baseball was wearing a helmet when he stepped to home plate.

ABOVE: Dale Long models the batting helmet worn by the Pirates in the early 1950s.   **RIGHT**: The famous Honus Wagner card.

How did the Pirates get their name?

LEGEND HAS IT that they "pirated" some of their players. In 1890, the Pittsburgh Alleghenys won only 23 games. The club's owners decided to dump the team and start a new one in 1891. They did this for many reasons, but mostly because it allowed the club to sign stars from other teams and leagues. Pittsburgh was later accused of taking players from their rightful owners. Soon the team became known as the Pirates.

Is Honus Wagner's baseball card the most valuable card in history?

LEGEND HAS IT that it is. In the early 1900s, baseball cards were packed with candy and also cigarettes. In 1909, a tobacco company printed Wagner's card without his permission. He said that he did not want to promote smoking and forced the company to stop printing his card. However, a few had already been made. Today the card is very rare. Some have been sold for more than $2 million.

WAGNER, PITTSBURG

It Really Happened

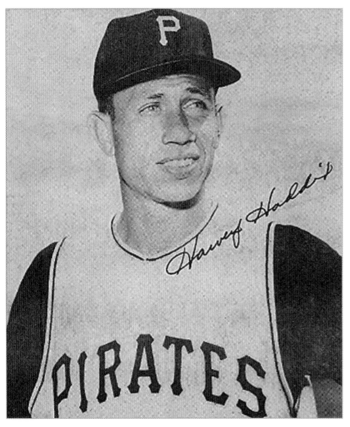

Harvey Haddix was one of the best young pitchers in baseball in the early 1950s. A line drive off the bat of Joe Adcock in 1954 nearly destroyed his knee. Haddix recovered, but he was never the same pitcher again—except for one chilly May night in Milwaukee against the Braves in 1959.

Inning after inning, the Braves went down 1–2–3. Haddix was throwing strikes, and the Milwaukee batters were hitting weak grounders and fly balls. The crowd began to realize that Haddix was working on a **perfect game**. They applauded for the opposing pitcher after each inning. When it started to drizzle in the seventh inning, only a few fans left their seats.

Milwaukee's starter, Lew Burdette, was also pitching well. He gave up a lot of hits, but the Pirates could not score. Haddix struck out Burdette to end the

ninth inning with a perfect game, but the score was still 0–0. Haddix would have to go back out to the mound.

Finally, in the 13th inning, the Braves put a man on base after a throwing error by the Pirates. The perfect game was gone. After the Braves bunted the runner to second base, Haddix walked slugger Henry Aaron. He was hoping to get the next batter, his old rival Adcock, to hit into a double play.

Unfortunately, Adcock slammed Haddix's second pitch over the right field wall to win the game. No one had ever pitched 12 perfect innings before. Poor Harvey had nothing to show for his effort but a loss.

LEFT: Harvey Haddix, who was perfect for 12 innings against the Milwaukee Braves but not 13.   **ABOVE**: A trading card marks Haddix's amazing performance.

Team Spirit

On game days in Pittsburgh, fans travel from all over the area to the ballpark. Some come by car and bus, others by riverboat, and thousands walk to the stadium. The city closes down Roberto Clemente Bridge so fans can stroll across it from downtown Pittsburgh.

Those fans come to root for the Pirates. They also come to the ballpark to have fun. There are restaurants, shops, and games to play in an area behind the stadium's right field wall. Fans also cheer for the team's **mascots**, the Pirate Parrot and Captain Jolly Roger.

Pirates fans are very loyal. They have supported the team through many ups and downs. When Pittsburgh is winning, there is not a better city for baseball. The fans love to show up for games ready to cheer loudly for their team.

Jason Bay signs autographs for the fans before the 2006 All-Star Game, which was held in Pittsburgh.

Timeline

Triple play.

TOMMY LEACH
PITTSBURG.

Tommy Leach, who led all hitters with a .360 average in the 1909 World Series.

1902
The Pirates rule the NL with a record of 103–36.

1909
The Pirates defeat the Detroit Tigers to win the World Series.

1946
Rookie Ralph Kiner leads the NL with 23 home runs.

1887
The team joins the NL after five years in the American Association.

1927
Paul and Lloyd Waner lead the Pirates to the pennant.

1937
First baseman Gus Suhr sets an NL record by playing 822 games in a row.

DUNLAP
(CAPT. PITTSBURG)

OLD JUDGE & GYPSY QUEEN CIGARETTES

Fred Dunlap, one of the team's first stars.

Gus Suhr

34

Kent Tekulve, whose pitching helped the Pirates win in 1979.

Freddy Sanchez

1960
The Pirates defeat the New York Yankees in the World Series.

1979
The Pirates defeat the Baltimore Orioles in the World Series.

2006
Freddy Sanchez wins the NL batting title.

1972
Roberto Clemente gets his 3,000th hit on the last day of the season.

1983
Bill Madlock wins his second batting title as a Pirate.

1990
Doug Drabek wins the NL **Cy Young Award**.

Roberto Clemente shows the ball from his 3,000th hit.

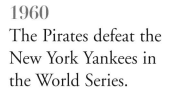

Bill Madlock

Fun Facts

NO PLACE LIKE HOME

The 1902 Pirates had a 56–15 record in Exposition Park. No NL team has ever been better at home.

23 SKIDDOO!

First baseman Charlie Grimm started the 1923 season with hits in each of his first 23 games.

NEW WAVE

In 1921, a Pittsburgh radio station made the first broadcast of a baseball game. The contest it covered was the Pirates against the Philadelphia Phillies.

CRAZY EIGHTS

In 1956, Dale Long became the first player to sock a home run in eight games in a row.

ABOVE: Charlie Grimm   **RIGHT**: Roy Face

NIGHT MOVES

In 1971, the first World Series night game was played in Pittsburgh's Three Rivers Stadium.

BAY WATCH

In the 1990 Little League World Series, a team from the tiny Canadian town of Trail beat powerful Mexico. The star of the Canadian team was 11-year-old Jason Bay.

HIGH JUMP

One of Pittsburgh's best pitchers during the 1880s was named Cannonball Morris. He would leap high off the mound and then fire the ball at the batter when he landed.

IN YOUR FACE

Roy Face was the best relief pitcher of his *era*. He won 22 games in a row in 1958 and 1959, and **saved** three games in the 1960 World Series. Face's best weapon was a sinking pitch called a forkball.

ROY **Face**
PITTSBURGH PIRATES PITCHER

Talking Baseball

HANS WAGNER
S. S.—Pittsburg Nationals
184

"I want to be remembered as a ballpayer who gave all he had to give."
—*Roberto Clemente, on always playing at full speed*

"I don't want my picture in any cigarettes."
—*Honus Wagner, on why he told a tobacco company not to print his baseball card*

"I'm always amazed when a pitcher becomes mad at a hitter for hitting a home run off him. When I strike out, I don't get angry at the pitcher—I get angry at myself!"
—*Willie Stargell, on dealing with failure on the field*

"If a pitcher sees you fiddling with the bat, he'll stall until your arms are tired before you ever get a chance to hit."
—*Paul Waner, on the importance of standing still in the batter's box*

"Home run hitters drive Cadillacs. Singles hitters drive Fords."
—*Ralph Kiner, on the players who make the highest salaries*

"Wherever they play me, I am ready for it. I might not know where I am until I check the **lineup** card every day, but I work hard and it will all fall into place."
—*Freddy Sanchez, on being ready to play different positions*

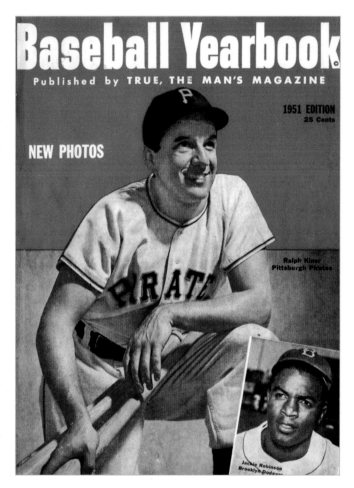

"This is everything I have been working for!"
—*Tom Gorzelanny, on being a winner in the big leagues*

LEFT: Honus Wagner, who was also called "Hans."
ABOVE: Ralph Kiner

For the Record

The great Pirates teams and players have left their marks on the record books. These are the "best of the best" …

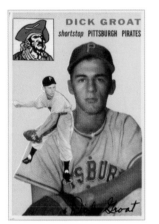

Dick Groat

Jason Bay

PIRATES AWARD WINNERS

WINNER	AWARD	YEAR
Vern Law	Cy Young Award	1960
Dick Groat	Most Valuable Player	1960
Roberto Clemente	Most Valuable Player	1966
Roberto Clemente	World Series MVP	1971
Dave Parker	Most Valuable Player	1978
Dave Parker	All-Star Game MVP	1979
Willie Stargell	co-Most Valuable Player	1979
Willie Stargell	World Series MVP	1979
Jim Leyland	Manager of the Year	1990
Doug Drabek	Cy Young Award	1990
Barry Bonds	Most Valuable Player	1990
Jim Leyland	Manager of the Year	1992
Barry Bonds	Most Valuable Player	1992
Jason Bay	Rookie of the Year	2004

Roberto Clemente

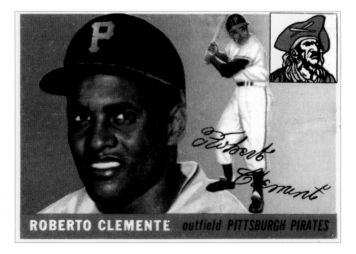

PIRATES ACHIEVEMENTS

ACHIEVEMENT	YEAR
NL Pennant Winners	1901
NL Pennant Winners	1902
NL Pennant Winners	1903
NL Pennant Winners	1909
World Series Champions	1909
NL Pennant Winners	1925
World Series Champions	1925
NL Pennant Winners	1927
NL Pennant Winners	1960
World Series Champions	1960
NL East Champions	1970
NL East Champions	1971
NL Pennant Winners	1971
World Series Champions	1971
NL East Champions	1972
NL East Champions	1974
NL East Champions	1975
NL East Champions	1979
NL Pennant Winners	1979
World Series Champions	1979
NL East Champions	1990
NL East Champions	1991
NL East Champions	1992

Interior Forbes Field, Pittsburgh, Pa.
PHOTO AND COPYRIGHT BY CHAUTAUQUA PHOTOGRAPHING CO., PITTSBURGH, PA.

TOP: Chuck Tanner talks to his players during the 1979 World Series.
ABOVE: Andy Van Slyke, a star in the early 1990s.
LEFT: Forbes Field, the Pirates' home from 1909 to 1970.

41

Pinpoints

The history of a baseball team is made up of many smaller stories. These stories take place all over the map—not just in the city a team calls "home." Match the pushpins on these maps to the Team Facts and you will begin to see the story of the Pirates unfold!

TEAM FACTS

1 Pittsburgh, Pennsylvania—*The Pirates have played here since 1883.*

2 Dover, Delaware—*Ian Snell was born here.*

3 Boston, Massachusetts—*Richie Hebner was born here.*

4 Cincinnati, Ohio—*Kent Tekulve was born here.*

5 Memphis, Tennessee—*Bill Madlock was born here.*

6 Winterset, Iowa—*Fred Clarke was born here.*

7 Meridian, Idaho—*Vern Law was born here.*

8 Earlsboro, Oklahoma—*Willie Stargell was born here.*

9 San Diego, California—*Jason Kendall was born here.*

10 Trail, British Columbia, Canada—*Jason Bay was born here.*

11 Colon, Panama—*Manny Sanguillen was born here.*

12 Carolina, Puerto Rico—*Roberto Clemente was born here.*

Jason Kendall

Play Ball

Baseball is a game played between two teams over nine innings. Teams take one turn at bat and one turn in the field during each inning. A turn at bat ends when three outs are made. The batters on the hitting team try to reach base safely. The players on the fielding team try to prevent this from happening.

In baseball, the ball is controlled by the pitcher. The pitcher must throw the ball to the batter, who decides whether or not to swing at each pitch. If a batter swings and misses, it is a strike. If the batter lets a good pitch go by, it is also a strike. If the batter swings and the ball does not stay in fair territory (between the v-shaped lines that begin at home plate) it is called "foul," and is counted as a strike. If the pitcher throws three strikes, the batter is out. If the pitcher throws four bad pitches before that, the batter is awarded first base. This is called a base-on-balls, or "walk."

When the batter swings the bat and hits the ball, everyone springs into action. If a fielder catches a batted ball before it hits the ground, the batter is out. If a fielder scoops the ball off the ground and throws it to first base before the batter arrives, the batter is out. If the batter reaches first base safely, he is credited with a hit. A one-base hit is called a single, a two-base hit is called a double, a three-base hit is called a triple, and a four-base hit is called a home run.

Runners who reach base are only safe when they are touching one of the bases. If they are caught between the bases, the fielders can tag them with the ball and record an out.

A batter who is able to circle the bases and make it back to home plate before three outs are made is credited with a run scored. The team with the most runs after nine innings is the winner.

Anyone who has played baseball (or softball) knows that it can be a complicated game. Every player on the field has a job to do. Different players have different strengths and weaknesses. The pitchers, batters, and managers make hundreds of decisions every game. The more you play and watch baseball, the more "little things" you are likely to notice. The next time you are at a game, look for these plays:

PLAY LIST

DOUBLE PLAY—A play where the fielding team is able to make two outs on one batted ball. This usually happens when a runner is on first base, and the batter hits a ground ball to one of the infielders. The base runner is forced out at second base and the ball is then thrown to first base before the batter arrives.

HIT AND RUN—A play where the runner on first base sprints to second base while the pitcher is throwing the ball to the batter. When the second baseman or shortstop moves toward the base to wait for the catcher's throw, the batter tries to hit the ball to the place that the fielder has just left. If the batter swings and misses, the fielding team can tag the runner out.

INTENTIONAL WALK—A play when the pitcher throws four bad pitches on purpose, allowing the batter to walk to first base. This happens when the pitcher would much rather face the next batter—and is willing to risk putting a runner on base.

SACRIFICE BUNT—A play where the batter makes an out on purpose so that a teammate can move to the next base. On a bunt, the batter tries to "deaden" the pitch with the bat instead of swinging at it.

SHOESTRING CATCH—A play where an outfielder catches a short hit an inch or two above the ground, near the tops of his shoes. It is not easy to run as fast as you can and lower your glove without slowing down. It can be risky, too. If a fielder misses a shoestring catch, the ball might roll all the way to the fence.

Glossary

BASEBALL WORDS TO KNOW

ALL-AROUND—Good at all parts of the game.

ALL-STARS—Players who are selected to play in baseball's annual All-Star Game.

AMERICAN ASSOCIATION (AA)—A rival to the National League in the 1800s. The AA played from 1882 to 1891.

AMERICAN LEAGUE (AL)—One of baseball's two major leagues; the AL began play in 1901.

CY YOUNG AWARD—The annual trophy given to each league's best pitcher.

DRAFTED—Selected at the annual meeting at which teams take turns choosing the best players in high school and college.

FREE AGENTS—Players who are allowed to join any team they want.

GOLD GLOVE—An award given each year to baseball's best fielders.

LINEUP—The list of players who are playing in a game.

MOST VALUABLE PLAYER (MVP)—An award given each year to each league's top player; an MVP is also selected for the World Series and All-Star Game.

NATIONAL LEAGUE (NL)—The older of the two major leagues; the NL began play in 1876.

NATIONAL LEAGUE CHAMPIONSHIP SERIES (NLCS)—The competition that has decided the National League pennant since 1969.

PENNANT—A league championship. The term comes from the triangular flag awarded to each season's champion, beginning in the 1870s.

PERFECT GAME—A full game in which a pitcher does not allow any batters to reach base.

RELIEF PITCHER—A pitcher who is brought into a game to replace another pitcher. Relief pitchers can be seen warming up in the bullpen.

ROOKIE OF THE YEAR—The annual award given to each league's best first-year player.

RUNS BATTED IN (RBI)—A statistic that counts the number of runners a batter drives home.

SAVED—Recorded the last out in a team's win. A pitcher on the mound for the last out of a close victory is credited with a "save."

SLIDER—A fast pitch that curves and drops just as it reaches the batter.

SLUGGERS—Powerful hitters.

SLUGGING AVERAGE—A statistic that helps measure a hitter's power. It is calculated by dividing the number of total bases a batter has by his official times at bat.

STARTING PITCHER—The pitcher who begins the game for his team.

THROW-IN—A player without much value who is added to a trade.

WORLD SERIES—The world championship series played between the winners of the National League and American League.

OTHER WORDS TO KNOW

AGILE—Quick and graceful.

CENTURY—A period of 100 years.

COMEBACK—The process of catching up from behind, or making up a large deficit.

DECADE—A period of 10 years; also specific periods, such as the 1950s.

DISCO—A style of music popular in the 1970s.

ENTHUSIASM—Strong excitement.

ERA—A period of time in history.

EVAPORATE—Disappear, or turn into vapor.

EXTRAORDINARY—Unusual or remarkable.

FLANNEL—A soft wool or cotton material.

GENERATION—A period of years roughly equal to the time it takes for a person to be born, grow up, and have children.

LOGO—A symbol or design that represents a company or team.

MASCOTS—Animals or people believed to bring a group good luck.

PATIENCE—Ability to wait calmly.

REMARKABLE—Unusual or exceptional.

STANDARD—A guide or example.

SYNTHETIC—Made in a laboratory, not in nature.

TRADITION—A belief or custom that is handed down from generation to generation.

UNCOILED—Released from a tense position.

Places to Go

ON THE ROAD

PITTSBURGH PIRATES
115 Federal Street
Pittsburgh, Pennsylvania 15212
(412) 321-BUCS

NATIONAL BASEBALL HALL OF FAME AND MUSEUM
25 Main Street
Cooperstown, New York 13326
(888) 425-5633
www.baseballhalloffame.org

ON THE WEB

THE PITTSBURGH PIRATES   www.pittsburghpirates.com
* *Learn more about the Pirates*

MAJOR LEAGUE BASEBALL   www.mlb.com
* *Learn more about all the major league teams*

MINOR LEAGUE BASEBALL   www.minorleaguebaseball.com
* *Learn more about the minor leagues*

ON THE BOOKSHELF

To learn more about the sport of baseball, look for these books at your library or bookstore:

* Kelly, James. *Baseball.* New York, New York: DK, 2005.

* Jacobs, Greg. *The Everything Kids' Baseball Book.* Cincinnati, Ohio: Adams Media Corporation, 2006.

* Stewart, Mark and Kennedy, Mike. *Long Ball: The Legend and Lore of the Home Run.* Minneapolis, Minnesota: Millbrook Press, 2006.

Index

PAGE NUMBERS IN **BOLD** REFER TO ILLUSTRATIONS.

The Team

MARK STEWART has written more than 25 books on baseball, and over 100 sports books for kids. He grew up in New York City during the 1960s rooting for the Yankees and Mets, and now takes his two daughters, Mariah and Rachel, to the same ball-parks. Mark comes from a family of writers. His grand-father was Sunday Editor of the *New York Times* and his mother was Articles Editor of *Ladies' Home Journal* and *McCall's*. Mark has profiled hundreds of athletes over the last 20 years. He has also written several books about his native New York and New Jersey, his home today. Mark is a graduate of Duke University, with a degree in history. He lives with his daughters and wife, Sarah, overlooking Sandy Hook, NJ.

JAMES L. GATES, JR. has served as Library Director at the National Baseball Hall of Fame since 1995. He had previously served in academic libraries for almost fifteen years. He holds degrees from Belmont Abbey College, the University of Notre Dame, and Indiana University. During his career Jim has authored several academic articles and has served in an editorial capacity on multiple book, mag-azine, and museum publications, and he also serves as host for the Annual Cooperstown Symposium on Baseball and American Culture. He is an ardent Baltimore Orioles fan and enjoys watching baseball with his wife and two children.